The Library of Cells™

Eukaryotic and Prokaryotic Cell Structures

Understanding Cells With and Without a Nucleus

Lesli J. Favor, Ph.D.

The Rosen Publishing Group, Inc., New York

For Steve

Published in 2005 by The Rosen Publishing Group, Inc.
29 East 21st Street, New York, NY 10010

Library of Congress Cataloging-in-Publication Data

Favor, Lesli J.
Eukaryotic and prokaryotic cell structures: understanding cells with and without a nucleus/by Lesli J. Favor.
    p. cm.—(The library of cells)
Includes bibliographical references and index.
ISBN 1-4042-0323-0 (library binding)
1. Cytology—Juvenile literature. 2. Eukaryotic cells—Juvenile literature. 3. Prokaryotes—Juvenile literature.
I. Title. II. Series.
QH582.5.F38 2005
571.6—dc22

                                                    2004016700

Manufactured in the United States of America

On the cover: This enhanced electron micrograph shows the individual organelles inside a eukaryotic plant cell, including its nucleus, Golgi apparatus, mitochondria, chloroplasts, endoplasmic reticulum, and fluid-filled vacuoles.

Contents

Introduction

If you have ever built a tower from building blocks, then you understand how small parts can work together to make a larger structure. Similarly, if you have ever taken apart a tower of blocks, you know what it means to find the smallest unit that makes up a larger structure. Living organisms are like that tower of blocks, except the blocks are cells. Cells are the building blocks of life.

All living things—animals, plants, fungi, protists, bacteria—are made up of one or more cells. These cells all have a similar structure, and it is a cell's genetic material that tells it how to function. For example, a bacterium is made up of a single cell. In contrast, each human has billions of cells in his or her body. Most cells are microscopic; they are too tiny for the human eye to see without a microscope. Thousands of bacteria cells, for example, could fit on the period at the end of this sentence. However, some cells can be seen with the naked eye. For example, if you crack open a hen's egg and examine the yolk, you are looking at one large cell.

The study of cells is a branch of biology called cytology. Scientists first studied cells in the

1660s. These first cytologists were Robert Hooke and Antonie van Leeuwenhoek. Hooke was the first scientist to use the word "cell." In 1665, he studied thin slices of cork under a microscope. To him, the tiny, boxlike sections of cork looked like cells, or rooms. In 1702, van Leeuwenhoek studied blood under a microscope, and he was the first scientist to describe red blood cells.

Cells have specific parts that perform specific functions. These cell parts make it possible for the cell to grow and divide, to produce proteins, to transform energy (such as sunlight), and to carry out specific tasks.

Each cell has a membrane that separates it from the outside world. Inside the cell is a mixture of thousands of different molecules, which perform a variety of specialized jobs. These parts carry out cell functions such as energy transformation, transfer of molecules, digestion, waste disposal, storage of genetic material, and so on.

All cells are either eukaryotic or prokaryotic. Eukaryotic cells have membrane-bound organelles ("little organs"). The cell's nucleus, for example, is an organelle. Prokaryotic cells do not have membrane-bound organelles. Within the prokaryotic cell membrane, cell parts float freely in the cytoplasm. Nuclear material, for example, is not closed off inside a nuclear membrane. Aside from this main difference, both cell groups have similar parts. This book explains in detail the structure and the parts of cells.

Chapter One

The Structure of a Typical Cell

In the late 1830s, two German scientists, Matthias J. Schleiden and Theodor Schwann, formed a theory about cells. Although the two researchers were not working together, each man came up with the same set of ideas. We call it the cell theory. The main points of cell theory are that the cell is the smallest unit of life, that all living things are made up of one or more cells, and that all cells come from the growth and division of cells that already exist.

Eukaryotes and Prokaryotes

All cells can be divided into two basic types. In eukaryotic cells, a membrane encloses the nucleus, and the nuclear material does not mix with the cytoplasm. These cells are called eukaryotes, and most cells belong to this category. In contrast, prokaryotic cells contain nuclear material that is not enclosed in a membrane. This nuclear material floats freely in the cytoplasm. All bacteria are prokaryotes.

In fact, the only prokaryotic life-forms are bacteria and cyanobacteria (blue-green algae). These two kinds of bacteria form the scientific kingdom

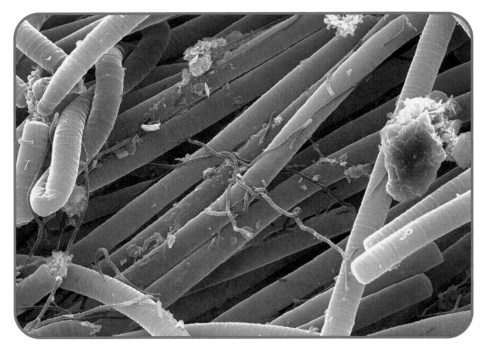

This scanning electron micrograph shows cyanobacteria, or typical blue-green algae. Algae are considered among Earth's most primitive organisms, dating back to the Precambrian era approximately 600 million years ago. Although scientists have witnessed algae sway backward and forward, the exact mechanism for the movement is not yet fully understood.

Monera. The other four kingdoms are made up of eukaryotic life-forms. These kingdoms are Protista, Fungi, Plantae, and Animalia.

All cells have similar parts that work together to keep the cell alive. They also help the cell perform its work. Eukaryotic cells are larger and more complex than prokaryotic cells. In particular, eukaryotic cells have a cell membrane, cytoplasm, and a nucleus. The cytoplasm contains many small organs called organelles. Just the way organs work in a human's body, the cell's organs keep it alive and help it perform its work. Human beings are composed of eukaryotic cells. Prokaryotic cells are smaller and less complex. They do not have a separate nucleus. Deoxyribonucleic acid (DNA) is a molecule that floats in the cytoplasm.

Cell Structure

Since the development of microscopes in the 1600s, scientists have found many ways to study the structure of cells. A typical cell is too tiny to see with the naked eye, much less to study. Therefore, scientists use compound microscopes and electron microscopes to learn about cells. With most microscopes, only a dead cell can be studied. The compound microscope,

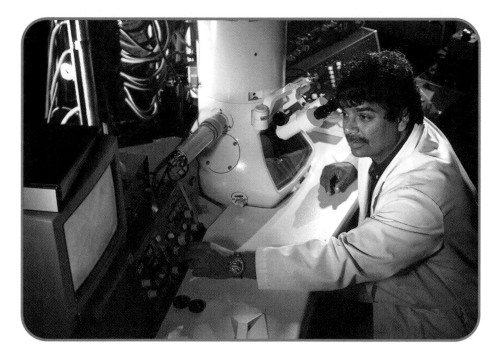

Professor Rajiv Singh is among the first scientists to use the field emission atomic chemical probe and microscope, the newest, most highly powered electron microscope in the United States. The new machine can examine specimens at the resolution of 1.4 angstroms, 400,000 times smaller than the diameter of a strand of human hair.

for example, uses light and two lenses to magnify a specimen. Scientists place an extremely thin specimen on the microscope's stage. Through the eyepiece, they study a magnified image of the specimen. Colored dyes used to stain the specimen cause parts of the cell to stand out more vividly than other parts.

Electron microscopes reveal a cell in even more detail. A transmission electron microscope sends a beam of electrons through a thinly sliced, stained specimen. (An electron is a tiny particle within an atom.) The resulting image, created on film, is called a transmission electron micrograph. To examine whole, nonsliced cells, scientists use a scanning electron microscope. It uses a vacuum chamber. In this chamber, electrons bounce off the surface of the cell. The resulting image is projected onto a video screen. A recent development, the scanning tunneling microscope allows scientists to examine living cells. This instrument uses a special probe that sends out electrons to skim the living cell's surface.

Using microscopes, scientists have learned that cells exist in various sizes and shapes. While plant cells often have straight sides and square corners, most animal cells are shaped more like balls. A blood cell looks like a slightly squashed ball with a thumbprint pressed into the center.

The size of cells is measured in microns. One micron equals one-millionth of a meter. About 25,000 microns equal one inch. Some cells are as

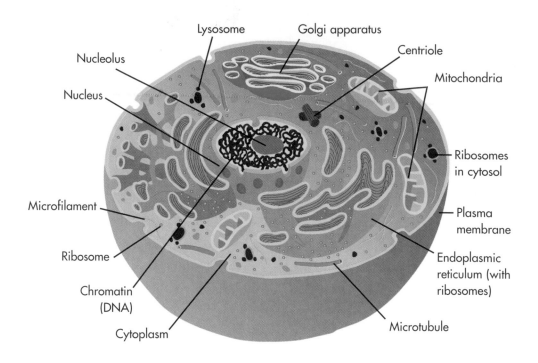

The organelles of a typical eukaryotic animal cell are shown in this diagram. Eukaryotic cells, or cells that contain a nucleus, are far more complex than prokaryotic cells, which do not contain a nucleus. Although the type of cell dictates the proportions of its organelles, all the information needed to determine these patterns is contained within the cell's DNA.

tiny as 0.2 microns in diameter. In the human body, most cells are about 10 microns in diameter.

Protoplasm

All cells are made up of protoplasm, a combination of water, electrolytes, proteins, lipids, and carbohydrates. You can think of these substances as the ingredients in the recipe for making a cell. Protoplasm forms the three main parts of a cell: the cell membrane, the cytoplasm, and the nucleus. Scientists call protoplasm the "living jelly." The nickname suggests facts about

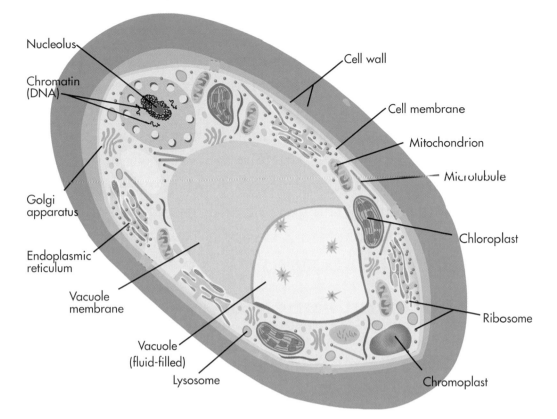

Nucleolus

Chromatin
(DNA)

Golgi
apparatus

Endoplasmic
reticulum

Vacuole
membrane

Vacuole
(fluid-filled)

Lysosome

Cell wall

Cell membrane

Mitochondrion

Microtubule

Chloroplast

Ribosome

Chromoplast

The organelles of a typical eukaryotic plant cell are shown in this diagram. The chloroplasts contain molecules of chlorophyll, the pigment that makes plants green. Chloroplasts are found only in plant cells. They are large green organelles that trap sunlight and use it to make food. This process, which creates oxygen as a waste product, is called photosynthesis.

protoplasm. First, it is a jelly-like substance. Second, it helps form life. These facts support the cell theory— living protoplasm forms living cells, and living cells form all living things.

All the main parts of a cell are formed of protoplasm. However, each main part has a separate purpose. You can think of the three parts as parts of an egg. The membrane is like the eggshell. The cytoplasm is like the egg white. And the nucleus is like the yolk. The cell membrane encloses all of the cell's parts. Inside the membrane is the cytoplasm, where most cell tasks are performed. Finally, there is the nucleus. In eukaryotic cells, the nucleus has its own membrane and is surrounded by cytoplasm. In prokaryotic cells, the nuclear material is not inside a membrane, and it floats within the cytoplasm. The nucleus controls the growth and heredity of the cell. In this book, chapters 2 through 4 give additional details about these main parts of cells.

Shapes and Functions

Cells exist in many different shapes. For example, some cells have a cube shape. Others are round. Some are flat, and others are rod shaped. The spirillum bacterium cell is spiral shaped, for instance. It causes Lyme disease. In contrast, the human skin cell is tiny and flat.

Cells have specific functions, or jobs. In single-celled organisms, the cell carries out all tasks relating to the life of that organism. In multicelled organisms, different cells perform different tasks, depending on the instructions from the DNA. Cells work together to form tissues and organs in animals, including humans. For instance, brain cells do different work than do liver cells. Skin cells and blood cells have different functions than heart cells do. In plants, cells form seeds, roots, stems, and fruits.

A cell's shape relates to its job. Flat skin cells link tightly together, making the skin a protective covering for the body. Part of the job of skin cells is keeping

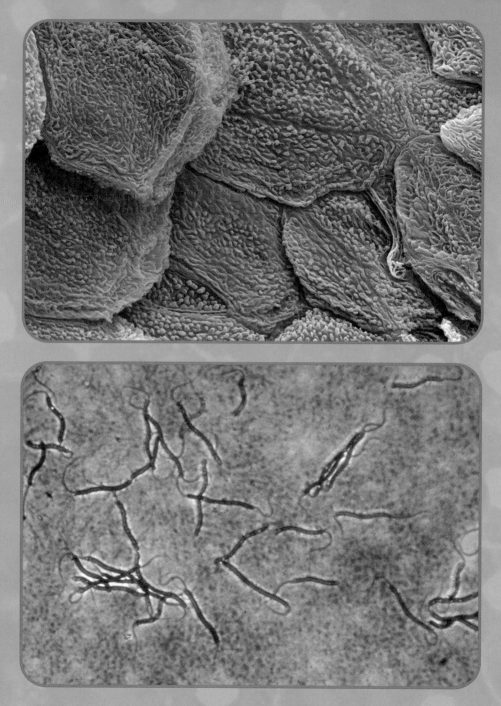

This micrograph of skin cells *(top)* was taken from the epidermis, or surface layer of human skin. This outer layer of skin cells is formed by a series of overlapping cells that are constantly dying and regenerating. Living cells from under the epidermis force newer, healthy cells toward the surface as others die off and are shed. The bottom micrograph shows the bacteria *Spirillum volutans.*

body fluids in and moisture from outside (such as rain) out. In addition, they form a barrier against germs. These flat skin cells do not move. In contrast, rounded blood cells move throughout the body. Their rounded shape helps them flow easily through blood vessels of all sizes.

One-Celled and Many-Celled Organisms

Some organisms are made up of just one cell, including bacteria and protozoans. They thrive in moist environments such as ponds, damp soil, lakes, oceans, and even inside other organisms. Bacteria are prokaryotes, which means they do not have a distinct nucleus. These microscopic cells are shaped like gumballs, corkscrews, and tiny ovals. Some bacteria use tiny, hairlike structures to propel themselves toward food or away from danger. Scientists believe that bacteria are probably the most numerous living things on our planet.

Thousands of species of protozoans exist. Of this huge group, the amoeba and the paramecium are perhaps the most familiar to students. The amoeba is a blob of jelly-like cytoplasm contained inside a cell membrane, with a tiny nucleus at its center. The cell's flexible membrane and soft cytoplasm allow it to continually move and change shape. The amoeba puts forward a pseudopod ("false foot"). Then the rest of the amoeba pours itself onto the pseudopod and returns to its former blob shape. To eat, the amoeba flows over a microscopic organism such as an alga or bacterium. It surrounds the food inside a pocket called a vacuole and digests it.

The paramecium is another one-celled eukaryote. Like all eukaryotic cells, the paramecium has a cell membrane, cytoplasm with organelles, and a membrane-bound nucleus. Unlike amoebas, however, paramecia are covered with short, hairlike cilia. These cilia help the cell move by waving, like soft

Tiny hairlike fibers called cilia, like those shown in this illustration, are found on paramecia, simple one-celled organisms. Tens of thousands of cilia project from the cell membrane and move in rotating formations in order to project the cell forward.

oars rowing a boat through water. Similar to amoebas, paramecia have vacuoles that digest food and expel waste.

Large plants and animals are many-celled. Millions or billions of cells make up each plant and animal. The cells themselves are usually microscopic. However, they work together to form muscle, tissues, bones, and organs. While one-celled organisms rely on cilia or pseudopods, for example, to move, animals have cells that work

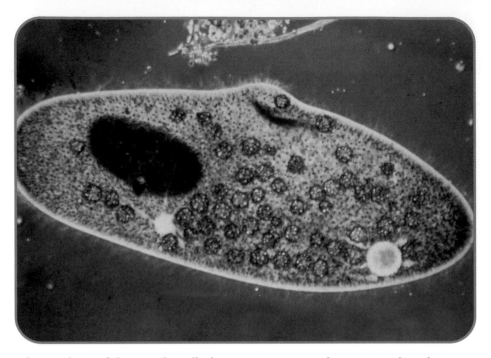

The nucleus of this single-celled paramecium can be seen in this electron micrograph. Paramecia are normally transparent green and live in freshwater streams, lakes, slow-moving rivers, or any other enclosed area that harbors fresh water.

together to form feet and legs for moving around. Whether single-celled or multicelled, all organisms have cytoplasm and genetic material. Most have cell membranes. These features are the focus of the following chapters in this book.

Chapter Two

The Cell Membrane

With a few exceptions, all cells have an outer "wrapper" that contains its parts and acts as a safety barrier against the outer world. The outer layer of the cell is called the cell membrane, or plasma membrane. Inside it are the cell's cytoplasm and its nuclear material. For many years, researchers have studied cell membranes, but they have not answered all their questions. They have, however, discovered a great deal about cell structure.

Although it serves as a defensive barrier to dangers, the cell membrane is extremely thin. It measures only about 10 nanometers in thickness. (One nanometer is one-billionth of a meter.) Despite its thin width, it is tough and flexible, like elastic. It is formed of a double layer of phospholipid molecules. (Phospholipids are similar to fat; they do not dissolve in water.) Protein molecules are set into these two layers. The cell membrane also has pores and caveolae (small "chambers" that gather chemical signals) in it, which help move molecules into and out of the cell.

Researchers have made educated guesses about the makeup of a cell membrane. A typical cell membrane is made up of about 60 percent protein and 40 percent lipids by weight. However, this is just an estimate. These numbers are different among different types of cells.

All cell membranes have a similar design. Lipid molecules form two membrane layers. Researchers use electron microscopes to see inside the cell membrane. They can see how the lipid molecules fit together. On one end, a lipid molecule is hydrophilic, or "water loving." The other end is hydrophobic, or "water fearing." In a cell membrane, the water-fearing ends of lipids face in toward one another. The water-loving ends face away from one another. Liquid inside and outside the cell helps stabilize the lipid layers. However, the water-fearing center of the membrane keeps liquids from flowing straight through the membrane.

The two layers of the membrane can

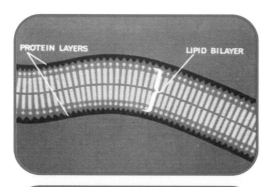

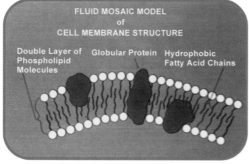

Detailed illustrations of a cellular membrane show its semipermeable structure. The cell's membrane serves as a protective outer layer to enclose the organelles, while it allows food inside the cell and forces waste out of it. This process is called transport.

move independently of one another. You can imagine this movement by placing the palms of your hands together and sliding them back and forth. This movement is like that of the two lipid layers in a membrane.

Protein molecules are set into the lipid layers. Some molecules are set into only one layer. Some reach across the middle to the other lipid layer. Each protein molecule can move within the membrane. The movements of proteins and lipids are signs of life. They are one reason why the cell membrane is sometimes called the living gatekeeper.

Just like other cell parts, the cell membrane has specific jobs to do. As mentioned earlier, protecting the cell from outside dangers is a key task. Besides that, the cell membrane is in charge of helping food and water enter the cell and allowing waste to exit. This work is like the job of a gatekeeper, another reason why the cell membrane has the nickname living gatekeeper.

Transport

The cell membrane is only partly penetrable. This means the "gatekeeper" does not let just anything cross the boundary. While it allows some molecules into the cell, it keeps others out. This trait is known as selective permeability, meaning the membrane selects which molecules it allows through the cell membrane. In this way, the membrane protects the cell from harmful substances.

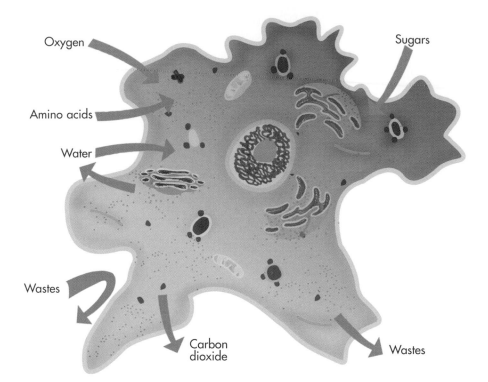

This diagram helps illustrate transport by selective permeability. Because the cell membrane selects what materials will enter and exit the cell, its contents are always changing to meet its needs. In doing so, the cell maintains a healthy balance, or homeostasis. In this image, oxygen, sugar (glucose), amino acids, and water enter the cell, while wastes such as nitrates and carbon dioxide are forced out.

In addition, the membrane can force out waste from the cell without losing valuable cell parts.

The movement of material in and out of the cell is called transport. Cells cannot survive without the processes of transport. Pores, globular proteins, phospholipids, and protoplasm all play a part in cell transport. First, pores in the membrane allow transport of small molecules. Second, caveolae in the membrane collect chemical signals and send them into

Contributions of Scientists

1665 Robert Hooke discovers plant cells.
1702 Antonie van Leeuwenhoek describes red blood cells.
1828 Robert Brown discovers the nucleus in an orchid cell.
1838 Matthias Schleiden and Theodor Schwann develop the cell theory.
1898 Camillo Golgi discovers the Golgi apparatus.
1945 Albert Claude and Keith Porter discover the endoplasmic reticulum.
1949 Christian de Duve discovers lysosomes.

the cell. Third, a process called diffusion helps larger molecules enter the cell. The more surface area the cell has, the more space there is to carry out transport.

The cell membrane has lots of folds and wrinkles in it. The wrinkles allow for more surface area. Imagine a smooth sheet of typing paper. One side of the paper has a surface area of 8½ by 11 inches. Now imagine wadding up the same-sized sheet. Although it seems much smaller, the wad of paper has the same surface area as the flat sheet. Cells are like the wadded-up paper. They have more surface area than their size suggests. This sizable surface area is useful to the cell. More food and water can reach the membrane at once. More space is available for chemical activities to occur. More exits are available for waste products.

Transport depends on liquid. Consequently, cells can survive only in the presence of liquid. The liquid brings food and water to the cell and carries away its waste. One-celled organisms usually exist in a body of water, in damp earth, or in moist areas of animals' bodies. Multicelled organisms depend on other liquid, too. Humans need blood, for example. Plants need sap. Blood and sap move throughout living organisms. They carry food to cells and carry away their waste.

A thick gel drips from the interior of this aloe vera plant. Beneath its thick green rind is an interior rich with fluid-filled vascular bundles of which the phloem and xylem are part. The phloem is a complex tissue system that helps plants transport starches from the roots to the leaves while the xylem transports water and minerals. The gel of the aloe plant has many healing properties and is commonly used to treat minor skin irritations and burns.

Plant Cell Walls

Unlike animal cells, plant cells have a thick wall surrounding the cell membrane. Like the cell membrane, the cell wall is permeable. It is made up of cellulose and protein that give the wall stiffness and strength. Cells link together to form sturdy plant parts. Think of the bark on a tree or the stem of a flower. Cellulose, working together with a fluid-filled pocket inside the cell, allows a plant to stand upright. Without cellulose, or without enough fluid in the vacuole, a trunk or stem would fall over.

The rigid nature of plant cells gives stability to plants, allowing them to remain in place as long as they are alive. Unlike plants, animals need to be flexible. Their cells do not need a stiff cell wall. Flexible cells give animals the abilities to walk around, breathe, and carry out other functions. Flexible cells allow humans to perform hundreds of voluntary and involuntary functions such as smiling, sneezing, blinking, eating, breathing, and running. While the flexible bodies of animals and humans rely on bones, formed of bone cells, to give them support, plants rely on cell walls, formed of cellulose and protein, to give them support.

Cell Movement

Some kinds of cells, particu-larly those of single-celled

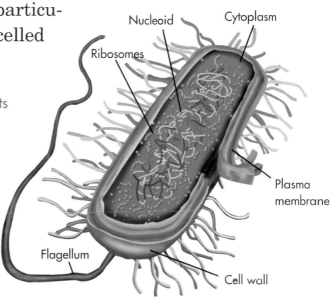

Nucleoid · Cytoplasm · Ribosomes · Plasma membrane · Flagellum · Cell wall

This diagram shows the parts of a rod-shaped bacterium. Instead of having a true nucleus, the DNA of this prokaryote floats freely in the cytoplasm, which is contained by the plasma membrane and cell wall. Its long fla-gellum helps propel it forward and backward.

organisms, have the ability to move around. Most mobile cells have either cilia or flagella to help them get to food, escape danger, or move for other reasons. Like hairs, cilia and flagella stick out from the cell membrane. However, they do not pierce the membrane. Rather, the membrane stretches to provide a protective cover. Cilia cluster in large numbers on a cell's surface. To move the cell, the cilia make waving motions, propelling the cell forward.

Flagella are longer than cilia, and they move like a snake swimming through water. Cells that move by means of flagella usually have only one or two of them. A good example is the sperm cell, with its long flagellum "tail." The salmonella bacterium, which can cause food poisoning in humans, has flagella that help it move.

In multicelled organisms, most cells stay in one place. However, some cells, such as human blood cells, move to carry out their tasks. Most cells, however, remain fixed in place, waiting for nutrients to come to them. The job of certain cells is to move fluids, such as blood or sap, over the surfaces of other cells. Although all cells have the same basic structure—a membrane, cytoplasm, and nuclear material—they perform different tasks according to instructions from their DNA. This valuable "blueprint" for the cell's purpose in life is one part of what exists in the cell's cytoplasm, the focus of the following chapter.

Chapter Three

Cytoplasm

Inside the cell wall is the cytoplasm, a clear or grayish gel-like substance. Cytoplasm is made up of water, proteins, carbohydrates, fats, and pigments (colors). The cytoplasm generally amounts to a little more than half the volume of an animal cell. It fills the area inside the cell wall and outside the nucleus. You can think of the cytoplasm as a busy factory where important tasks are continually carried out. The factory workers are organelles. They perform tasks called chemical reactions.

"Organelle" is a word that means "little organ." The organelles in a cell's cytoplasm control the overall function of the cell. Organelles make proteins and other materials, store materials, transform energy, and govern cell reproduction. Of course, prokaryotic cells do not have membrane-bound organelles. Instead, the chemical reactions of the prokaryotic cell take place in the cytoplasm.

Production of Materials

One of the most important jobs of the organelles is to make materials such as proteins and lipids (fats). The endoplasmic reticulum is key to this

Like a maze, the endoplasmic reticulum is the cell's organelle responsible for making proteins and secreting lipids (fats). Many of the cell's manufactured substances move through the endoplasmic reticulum before being stored in the cell's Golgi apparatus.

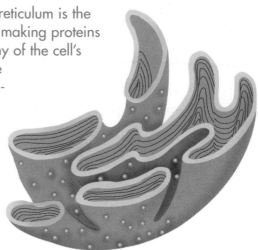

production. Its broad surface provides lots of space on which chemical reactions can take place. However, like a sheet of paper folded into many layers, the large surface area is folded into a tight network of thin membranes. If you have ever folded a sheet of paper into a fan, you can imagine how the endoplasmic reticulum might look.

Viewed through an electron microscope, some of the endoplasmic reticulum's surface appears bumpy. These "bumps" are actually ribosomes. Areas of the endoplasmic reticulum dotted with ribosomes are called "rough," while the areas without ribosomes are called "smooth." Besides dotting the surface of the endoplasmic reticulum, ribosomes float free within the cytoplasm. You can think of ribosomes as workstations where proteins are made.

The endoplasmic reticulum contains most of the enzymes necessary for the cell's production of lipids. Therefore, the chemical reactions to make lipids occur on its surface.

Besides being the site of protein and lipid production, the endoplasmic reticulum is a delivery system for the cell. The organelle is attached to the outer membrane of the nucleus, and its membranes stretch into the cytoplasm like thin, curvy roads. The folds in the membranes create a series of linked compartments.

Storage and Modification of Materials

Other organelles within the cytoplasm—the Golgi apparatus, vacuoles, and lysosomes—store and modify (change) proteins and lipids. They make sure that the cell has food for energy, that waste material such as excess water is collected and released, and that certain materials are digested.

The Golgi apparatus is a series of stacked, flat, pocketlike sacs. Viewed from the side with an electron

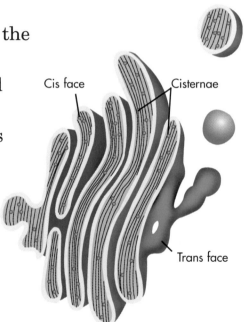

Cis face

Cisternae

Trans face

The flattened sacs of a eukaryotic cell's Golgi apparatus look like deflated balloons. The Golgi apparatus modifies and sorts the cell's proteins and lipids (fats). Its cis face is situated near the endoplasmic reticulum, while its trans face is beyond it. The Golgi apparatus is named after its discoverer, Camillo Golgi.

microscope, they resemble a stack of hollow pancakes. The job of these sacs is to store the proteins and lipids that are made on the surface of the endoplasmic reticulum. But this storage is only temporary. The other part of the Golgi apparatus's job is to release the proteins and lipids to the cell membrane and to other organelles.

Vesicles are a vital link between the endoplasmic reticulum and the Golgi apparatus. Vesicles are protein-filled pouches formed by breaking off the surface of the endoplasmic reticulum. The tiny pouches carry the proteins from the endoplasmic reticulum to the Golgi apparatus.

In a chemical reaction, the Golgi apparatus modifies the protein. It then sorts the proteins and places them in new vesicles. Next, these vesicles carry the proteins to various parts of the cell. At this point, the proteins may be incorporated, or fitted, into cell structures. Some are stored for later use, or, in the case of hormones and digestive enzymes, forced out of the cell as waste.

Another organelle whose purpose is storage is the vacuole. Vacuoles are fluid-filled, membrane-bound sacs within the cytoplasm. They store food, enzymes, and other materials until the cell needs them. Some vacuoles store worn-out cell parts or harmful viruses or bacteria until they can be expelled from the cell. In some single-celled organisms, vacuoles collect excess water and pump it out of the cell. A plant cell has one large vacuole that stores water and other materials. An animal cell usually contains many smaller vacuoles, which store various materials.

Lysosomes are organelles that contain enzymes (complex proteins) whose purpose is to digest. They help keep the cell alive by digesting food and worn-out or unneeded cell parts. For example, to digest the waste material stored in a vacuole, the lysosome combines itself with the vacuole and releases enzymes into it. The enzymes go to work, breaking down the stored material. In addition, lysosomes protect the cell by digesting harmful bacteria or viruses.

The lysosome's membrane keeps the enzymes from leaking into the cytoplasm and destroying important proteins. However, in some cases, lysosomes break down the cell that contain them. This digestion serves a special purpose. For example, when a tadpole changes into a frog, lysosomes digest the cells of the tadpole's tail. The molecules are then recycled in the production of new cells.

Energy Transformation

Every cell needs energy in order to function. In eukaryotic cells, membrane-bound organelles transform energy for the cell's use. To transform means to change the form of, or convert. In other words, the organelles do not create energy; rather, they convert energy into a form the cell can use.

In eukaryotic cells (but not in prokaryotic cells), mitochondria perform energy processing. In these organelles, food particles such as glycogen and fats

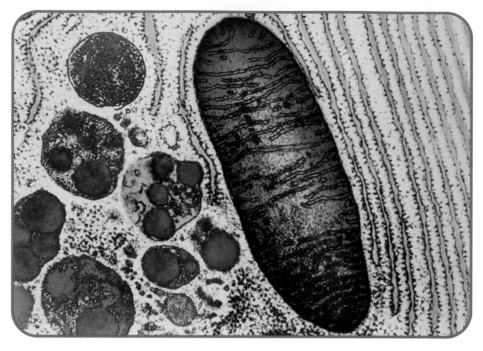

This electron micrograph shows a red-colored mitochondrion, the cell's organelle responsible for energy production. Mitochondria provide cells with energy by oxidizing glucose (sugar) and lipids (fats). Because they have both an inner membrane (the folds of which are called cristae) and an outer membrane, the surface areas of mitochondria are large.

are broken down, and this process releases energy. The energy is captured in molecules called ATP (adenosine triphosphate). Like a taxi, ATP carries the energy to where it is needed within the cell. ATP then releases the energy to fuel cell processes. According to Arthur C. Guyton, MD, author of *Textbook of Medical Physiology*, the mitochondria are responsible for 95 percent of the cell's energy supply. Numerous mitochondria are in each cell's cytoplasm. Liver cells contain some of the highest numbers of mitochondria, with up to 2,500 in each cell.

Mitochondria are rod shaped or thread shaped. Within the outer membrane is an inner membrane with lots of long folds called cristae. These cristae are coated with enzyme systems that help produce ATP. Just as the endoplasmic reticulum has a broad surface area packed into a small space thanks to many folds, each mitochondrion's inner membrane has a large surface area folded into a small space.

Energy transformation in the cells of green plants and some protists (prokaryotic cells) works a little differently. These cells have organelles called chloroplasts that take in sunlight and transform it into chemical energy. This chemical energy is stored in food mole-cules, including

1. Chloroplasts trap light energy

Light energy

2. Water enters leaf

4. Sugar leaves leaf

3. Carbon dioxide enters leaf through stomata

Photosynthesis (the process by which plants make sugar from sunlight, water, and carbon dioxide) is illustrated in this diagram of a plant leaf. Plant cells use chlorophyll-containing chloroplasts to absorb sunlight. Plant cells then use this energy to make food. Plants also absorb carbon dioxide to make food. Photosynthesis produces oxygen as a waste material that is then emitted through a plant's leaves.

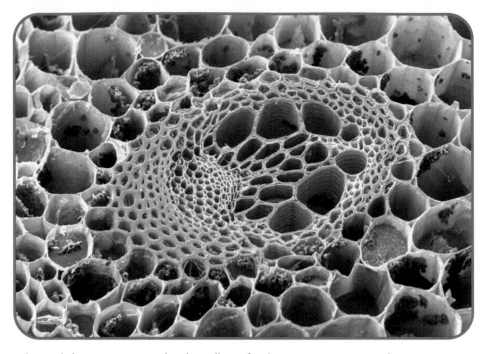

The tightly woven vascular bundles of a buttercup stem can be seen in this electron micrograph. The vascular bundle contains large xylem vessels *(center right)* that transport water from the roots to the stems. The phloem vessels that transport nutrients are colored orange.

sugars and starches. This energy transformation is possible because of molecules of chlorophyll. Chlorophyll, which is a green pigment, traps energy from sunlight. It also gives plants their green color.

Chloroplasts have a double-layer outer membrane and a folded inner membrane system called thylakoid membranes. Within the thylakoid membranes, energy from sunlight is trapped and transformed. The folds of the thylakoid membranes contain sacs. They are arranged in such a way that the sacs stack like buttons. These round, flat sacs are called grana. Surrounding the grana is fluid called stroma.

Chloroplasts are members of a group of plant organelles called plastids. Plastids store starches, lipids, or pigments (molecules that give color). Different plastids have different names, depending on the color of pigment they contain. For example, chloroplasts have a green color. Think of green leaves on trees and of green vegetables such as broccoli, spinach, and some peppers. Other plastids have colors such as those found in fruits and vegetables. When you think of red apples, orange carrots, blueberries, and yellow corn, you should understand that all of these plants get their color at the cellular level, in plastids.

Cytoskeleton

For many decades, scientists thought the organelles of a cell simply floated within the cytoplasm. However, within the past thirty years, scientists discovered a kind of skeleton of the cell, called the cytoskeleton. It makes up a frame, or support system, for the cell. In a similar way, a bony skeleton provides the support system for a human body. Unlike a bony skeleton, however, the cytoskeleton is flexible and can change its shape.

The cytoskeleton is mainly formed of microtubules and microfilaments. Microtubules are thin, hollow cylinders, and microfilaments are thin, solid fibers. When seen through an electron microscope, the network of microfilaments resembles a thick web. Both microtubules and microfilaments are made of protein.

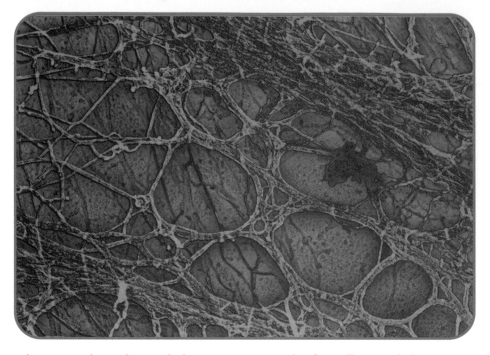

This is a color-enhanced electron micrograph of a cell's cytoskeleton. The cytoskeleton is made up of protein filaments that maintain the cell's shape, anchor organelles in place, and move parts of the cell in various processes that promote growth and movement.

In animal cells, an area called the centrosome is located next to the nucleus. The centrosome is spherical, like a basketball. In it is a pair of rod-shaped organelles called centrioles. Asters, or tiny tubules, stick out from the centrosome near the ends of the centrioles. Scientists have observed centrosomes and centrioles only in animal cells. However, they believe that plant cells have similar parts. Based on instructions from the cell's DNA, centrioles have a role in cell reproduction. DNA itself is located in the central organelle within the cytoplasm, the nucleus.

Chapter Four

The Nucleus

Like the Golgi apparatus and mitochondria, the nucleus is an organelle in the cell's cytoplasm. As you learned in chapter 3, organelles each serve a purpose in keeping the cell alive and functional. The nucleus is the control center of each cell. It is in charge of the cell's function and characteristics. If you think of all the organelles as a team within the cell, the nucleus would be the team captain. In eukaryotic cells, the nucleus is bound by a membrane. However, in prokaryotic cells, the nucleic material is concentrated in an area of the cytoplasm called the nucleoid.

Structure and Function

The nucleus, which is round or oval in shape, is located near the center of the cell, like the yolk in the center of a hen's egg. The nucleus manages the growth, division, and hereditary characteristics of the cell.

The nucleus is enclosed by a membrane, which is sometimes called the nuclear envelope. This membrane is formed of two double layers, one inside the other. Scientists believe that the

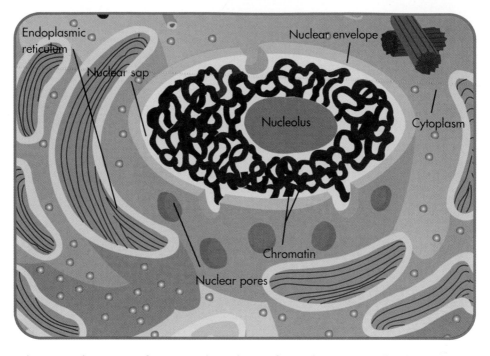

Endoplasmic reticulum

Nuclear sap

Nuclear envelope

Nucleolus

Cytoplasm

Chromatin

Nuclear pores

This is a diagram of a typical nucleus of a eukaryotic cell. The nucleus is surrounded by a double membrane, which protects the cell's chromatin (DNA) material. The double membrane is penetrated by nuclear pores that allow molecules to enter and exit the nucleus. Scientists believe that the nucleus is connected to the endoplasmic reticulum. Both are surrounded by cytoplasm.

outer membrane is connected to the endoplasmic reticulum, the network of membranes running throughout the cytoplasm and to the cell membrane. The inner nuclear membrane connects to a liquid called nucleoplasm.

If you've ever studied your face in a mirror, you have probably noticed the pores in your skin. Similarly, the nuclear membrane is dotted with thousands of pores. At almost 100 nanometers in diameter, each pore is relatively large. However, protein molecules line the edge of each pore, pushing into the opening to such an extent that the open area is less than 10 nanometers in diameter. Pores occur at places where both membranes meet and fuse (bind) together. Each one is an opening like a doorway through which materials pass in and out of the nucleus.

While scientists understand much about the nuclear membrane, they have not solved all of its puzzles. For example, scientists have observed molecules passing through pores more slowly than they would if the pore were simply a hole. The pores seem to have some control over the speed at which substances pass through them. However, scientists are still unsure how pores actually control the movement of substances.

Running throughout the nucleoplasm are thin threads of chromatin. Chromatin is formed of strands of DNA coated with proteins. A long series of genes, which are made up of DNA, forms each of these strands of DNA. Thus, chromatin contains genes. Genes determine the functions and traits of a cell. In particular, they hold hereditary (genetic) information. When the cell is ready to divide, chromatin condenses into chromosomes.

RNA

Genes control the production of ribonucleic acid (RNA), which is involved in making proteins in the cell. Various types of RNA exist. Ribosomal RNA helps make up ribosomes, which control the production of proteins in the cytoplasm. Messenger RNA carries a copy of the genetic code to the site of

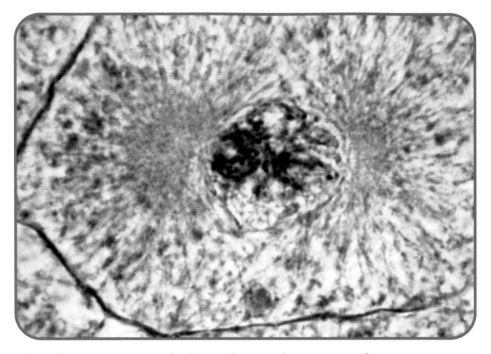

This electron micrograph shows the prophase stage of mitosis in an animal cell. During this stage, the cell's nuclear material disperses, its chromatin (DNA) begins to coil, and the centrosomes move away from each other toward opposite ends of the cell.

protein production on ribosomes. Transfer RNA brings specific amino acids that are needed in the proteins.

Scientists believe that RNA is produced in the inner part of the nucleus called the nucleolus. A nucleus has at least one nucleolus. When RNA is needed for the making of protein, it passes out of the nucleus through pores in the nuclear envelope. It travels to the ribosomes in the cytoplasm, where protein production takes place. Ribosomes form proteins according to the instructions given them by messenger RNA. For instance, human cells make only human proteins.

Cell Growth and Division

Every living thing begins its life as a single cell. Some organisms are unicellular, which means they have only one cell. Once the cell grows to full size, it divides into two "daughter" cells that are identical but separate. Each of these cells lives its own life. Protists, for example, are unicellular, and they live out their lives as a single cell.

Other organisms are multicellular, or many-celled. They, too, begin life as a single cell, but they quickly grow to include many cells. Once the original cell grows to full size, it divides. The two daughter cells are identical, and they remain joined, forming a

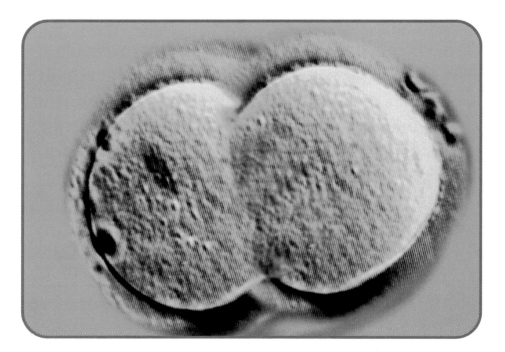

A cell is shown in the process of dividing in this micrograph. Cell division occurs when a cell divides to generate two daughter cells, each containing the exact same genetic material as the original cell.

tissue. A tissue is a group of cells working together for a purpose. For example, the bicep in your arm is a muscle tissue. A group of tissues working together for a purpose is an organ. Your stomach, liver, and eyes are examples of organs.

As the number of cells multiplies in an organism, the organism grows larger. A five-year-old child, for instance, does not have as many cells in his or her body as a fifteen-year-old teenager does. A kitten does not have as many cells as a full-grown cat. The same is true for plants—a bean sprout is made up of fewer cells than a full-grown vine.

Whether a cell is eukaryotic or prokaryotic, DNA gives the cell instructions on how to grow and divide, and what purpose to serve. Plant cells have DNA with instructions for making a plant, while animal cells have animal DNA. All cells, therefore, are similar in that they have a cell membrane, cytoplasm, and nuclear material including DNA. The DNA determines the cell's purpose in life. All life begins with a single cell, which, in turn, came from a preexisting cell. In this way, the cell is the basic unit of life.

Glossary

amoeba (uh-MEE-buh) A one-celled protozoan with a pseudopod, or "false foot."

caveolae (kah-VEE-oh-lay) Small enclosures of the plasma membrane that appear in most cell types, except neurons; a Latin word meaning "little caves."

cell (SEL) The smallest unit of independent life.

cell membrane (SEL MEM-brayn) The outer "envelope" of a cell. Also called the plasma membrane.

cell theory (SEL THEER-ee) A set of ideas about cells that was formed independently by Matthias J. Schleiden and Theodor Schwann in the late 1830s. It states that cells are the smallest unit of life, that all living things are made of one or more cells, and that all cells come from the growth and division of cells that already exist.

centrosome (SEN-tro-zome) A spherical area inside animal cells that is located next to the nucleus and contains a pair of rod-shaped organelles called centrioles.

chloroplast (KLOR-uh-plast) An organelle inside plant cells that takes in sunlight and transforms it to chemical energy during a process called photosynthesis; member of a group of organelles called plastids.

chromosome (KROH-muh-sohm) Particle in a cell that contains DNA.

cilia (SIH-lee-uh) The microscopic hairlike fibers on a cell's surface that allow it to move.

cyanobacteria (SY-ah-no-bac-teer-ee-uh) The scientific name for blue-green algae.

cytology (sy-TOL-oh-gee) The study of cells.

cytoplasm (SY-toe-plah-zum) All cell material in the space between the membrane and the nucleus.

cytoskeleton (SY-toe-skel-uh-tin) The "skeleton" inside the cell that helps support it.

DNA (deoxyribonucleic acid) (dee-ahk-see-rye-boh-noo-klay-ic AH-sid) The hereditary information for a cell.

endoplasmic reticulum (EN-do-plahs-mik reh-TIH-kyoo-lum) The network of membranes in the cytoplasm of eukaryotic cells.

enzyme (EN-zyme) A complex protein inside the lysosome.

eukaryote (YOO-kah-ree-oht) A cell that has a membrane-bound nucleus and membrane-bound organelles. All cells except bacteria are eukaryotes.

flagella (fluh-JEL-uh) A long microscopic "tail" on the surface of a cell that allows it to move.

gene (JEEN) A tiny part of a chromosome; it holds hereditary information for a cell.

Golgi apparatus (GOHL-gee ah-pahr-AH-tus) A cell structure that packages proteins and other substances the cell makes. Also called the Golgi body or Golgi complex.

lysosome (LY-so-zohm) A small cell part that contains enzymes for digestion.

micron (MY-kron) A unit of measure for one-millionth of a meter.

mitochondrion (MY-toh-kon-dree-un) A cell part in which respiration (breathing) takes place. Mitochondria produce most of the cell's energy. The plural of mitochondrion is mitochondria.

molecule (MAH-lih-kyul) A microscopic configuration of atomic nuclei and electrons that are bound together in a stable way.

nucleolus (NOO-klee-oh-lus) The part of the nucleus where DNA is read.

nucleoplasm (NOO-klee-oh-plah-zum) A liquid inside the inner nucleic membrane.

nucleus (NOO-klee-us) The cell part that stores hereditary information.

organelle (OR-gan-ell) Little organ; the name given to the parts of a cell that carry out tasks.

pore (POHR) The opening in a membrane that lets molecules pass through.

prokaryote (PRO-kayr-ee-oht) A cell whose nuclear material is not contained in a membrane. All bacteria arc prokaryotes.

protoplasm (PRO-toh-plah-zum) The basic substance that makes up all parts of a cell.

protozoan (pro-toh-ZOH-un) A one-celled organism such as the amoeba; protist.

pseudopod (SU-doh-pod) A "false foot" that extends from the amoeba, allowing the one-celled organism to reach food or escape danger.

ribosome (RY-boh-zohm) The cell part that makes proteins from amino acids.

RNA (ribonucleic acid) (RYE-boh-noo-klay-ik AH-sid) Nucleic acid involved in making proteins in the cell.

vacuole (VAK-u-ohl) Fluid-filled pocket bound by a membrane inside a cell.

For More Information

The American Society for Cell Biology
8120 Woodmont Avenue, Suite 750
Bethesda, MD 20814
(301) 347-9300
e-mail: ascbinfo@ascb.org
Web site: http://www.ascb.org

American Society of Cytopathology
400 West 9th Street, Suite 201
Wilmington, DE 19801
(302) 429-8802
e-mail: asc@cytopathology.org
Web site: http://www.cytopathology.org

Cell Transplant Society
Central Business Office
205 Viger Avenue West, Suite 201
Montreal, Quebec, Canada H2Z 1G2
(514) 874-1998
e-mail: info@celltx.org
Web site: http://www.celltx.org

Web Sites

Due to the changing nature of Internet links, the Rosen
Publishing Group, Inc., has developed an online list of
Web sites related to the subject of this book. This site is
updated regularly. Please use this link to access the list:

http://www.rosenlinks.com/lce/epcs

For Further Reading

Ball, Jacqueline A., ed. *Cells*. Milwaukee, WI: Gareth
    Stevens Publishing, 2003.

Bottone, Frank G. *The Science of Life: Projects and
    Principles for Beginning Biologists*. Chicago: Chicago
    Review Press, 2001.

Favor, Lesli. *Bacteria*. New York: The Rosen Publishing
    Group, 2004.

Ruiz, Andres Llamas. *The Life of a Cell*. New York:
    Sterling, 1997.

Snedden, Robert. *Diversity of Life: From Single Cells to
    Multicellular Organisms.* Chicago: Heinemann, 2003.

Snedden, Robert. *The World of the Cell: Life on a Small
    Scale*. Chicago: Heinemann, 2003.

Bibliography

Biggs, Alton, Chris Kapicka, and Linda Lundgren.
    Biology: The Dynamics of Life. New York: Glencoe
    McGraw-Hill, 1998.

Guyton, Arthur C. "The Cell and Its Function." *Textbook
    of Medical Physiology*. Eighth ed. Philadelphia: W. B.
    Saunders, 1991. pp. 9–23.

Johnson, George B. Biology: *Visualizing Life*. Orlando, FL:
    Holt, Rinehart and Winston, 1998.

Index

A
amoebas, 14–15
ATP, 30, 31

B
bacteria, 4, 6–7, 14, 15,
    24, 28

C
cell membrane, 10, 11–12,
    16, 17–24, 36, 40
  in amoebas, 14
  design of, 18–19
  in eukaryotic cells, 6, 7,
    12, 15
  functions of, 19
  makeup of, 17–18
  in paramecia, 15
cells
  division of, 39
  early study of, 4–5
  functions of, 5, 12–14,
    15–16
  growth of, 39–40
  movement of, 23–24
  shapes of, 12–14
  structure of, 6–16, 24
cell theory, 6, 11
cellulose, 22–23
centrosome, 34
chemical reactions,
    25–26, 28
chloroplasts, 31–33
chromatin, 37

cilia, 15, 16, 24
cytology, 4–5
cytoplasm, 5, 10, 11–12, 16,
    17, 24, 25–34, 35, 36,
    38, 40
  in amoebas, 14
  in eukaryotic cells, 6, 7,
    12, 15
  in paramecia, 15
  in prokaryotic cells, 6, 8,
    12, 25
cytoskeleton, 33

D
DNA, 8, 12, 24, 34, 37, 40

E
endoplasmic reticulum,
    25–27, 28, 31, 36
energy transformation,
    29–32
eukaryotes, 6, 7, 15, 29
eukaryotic cells, 5, 6, 7, 15
  nucleus and, 12, 35

G
Golgi apparatus,
    27–28, 35

H
Hooke, Robert, 5, 21

L
lysosomes, 27, 29

About the Author

Lesli J. Favor received her BA in English from the University of Texas at Arlington and then earned her MA and Ph.D. in English from the University of North Texas. She has also written *Bacteria*; *Women Doctors and Nurses of the Civil War*; *A Historical Atlas of America's Manifest Destiny*, and other books on science, biography, and history. She lives in Dallas, Texas, with her husband, two dogs, and horse.

Photo Credits

Cover, p.1 © Biophoto Associates/Photo Researchers, Inc.; pp. 7, 13 (top), 32 © Andrew Syred/Photo Researchers, Inc.; p. 8 © AP/Wide World Photos; pp. 10, 11, 15, 20, 23, 26, 27, 31, 36 by Tahara Anderson; p. 13 (bottom) © Michael Abbey/Photo Researchers, Inc.; p. 16 © Eric V. Grave/Photo Researchers, Inc.; p. 18 © 2000–2004 Custom Medical Stock Photo; p. 22 © Martin Harvey; Gallo Images/Corbis; p. 30 © Keith R. Porter/Photo Researchers, Inc.; p. 34 © Don W. Fawcett/ Photo Researchers, Inc.; p. 38 © Science Source/Photo Researchers, Inc.; p. 39 © Joubert/Photo Researchers, Inc.

Designer: Tahara Anderson; **Editor:** Joann Jovinelly